WELBECK
CHILDREN'S BOOKS

First published in Great Britain in 2025 by Welbeck Children's Books
An imprint of Hachette Children's Group
Text © 2025 Simon Mugford
Design & Illustration © 2025 Dan Green
Text for this edition adapted by Hannah Dolan

ISBN: 978-1-80453-821-0

Dan Green and Simon Mugford have asserted their moral rights to be identified as the illustrator and author of this Work in accordance with the Copyright Designs and Patents Act 1988.

All rights reserved. This book is sold subject to the condition that it may not be reproduced, stored in a retrieval system or transmitted in any form or by any means, electronic, mechanical, photocopying, recording, or otherwise, without the publisher's prior consent.

Writer: Simon Mugford
Designer and Illustrator: Dan Green
Designer: Arvind Shah
Design Manager: Sam James
Senior Commissioning Editor: Suhel Ahmed
Production: Melanie Robertson

Printed in China
10 9 8 7 6 5 4 3 2 1

Disclaimer: All names, characters, trademarks, service marks, and trade names referred to herein are the property of their respective owners and are used solely for identification purposes. This book is a publication of Hachette Children's Group and has not been licensed, approved, sponsored, or endorsed by any person or entity.

A CIP catalogue record for this book is available from the British Library.

Welbeck Children's Books
An imprint of Hachette Children's Group
Part of Hodder & Stoughton Limited
Carmelite House, 50 Victoria Embankment
London EC4Y 0DZ

The authorised representative in the EEA is Hachette Ireland, 8 Castlecourt Centre, Dublin 15, D15 XTP3, Ireland (email: info@hbgi.ie)

An Hachette UK Company
www.hachette.co.uk
www.hachettechildrens.co.uk

Football Stories

BRONZE

SIMON MUGFORD

DAN GREEN

Meet Lucy Bronze! She's one of the best players in women's football and an inspiration to young footballers. This book is all about her.

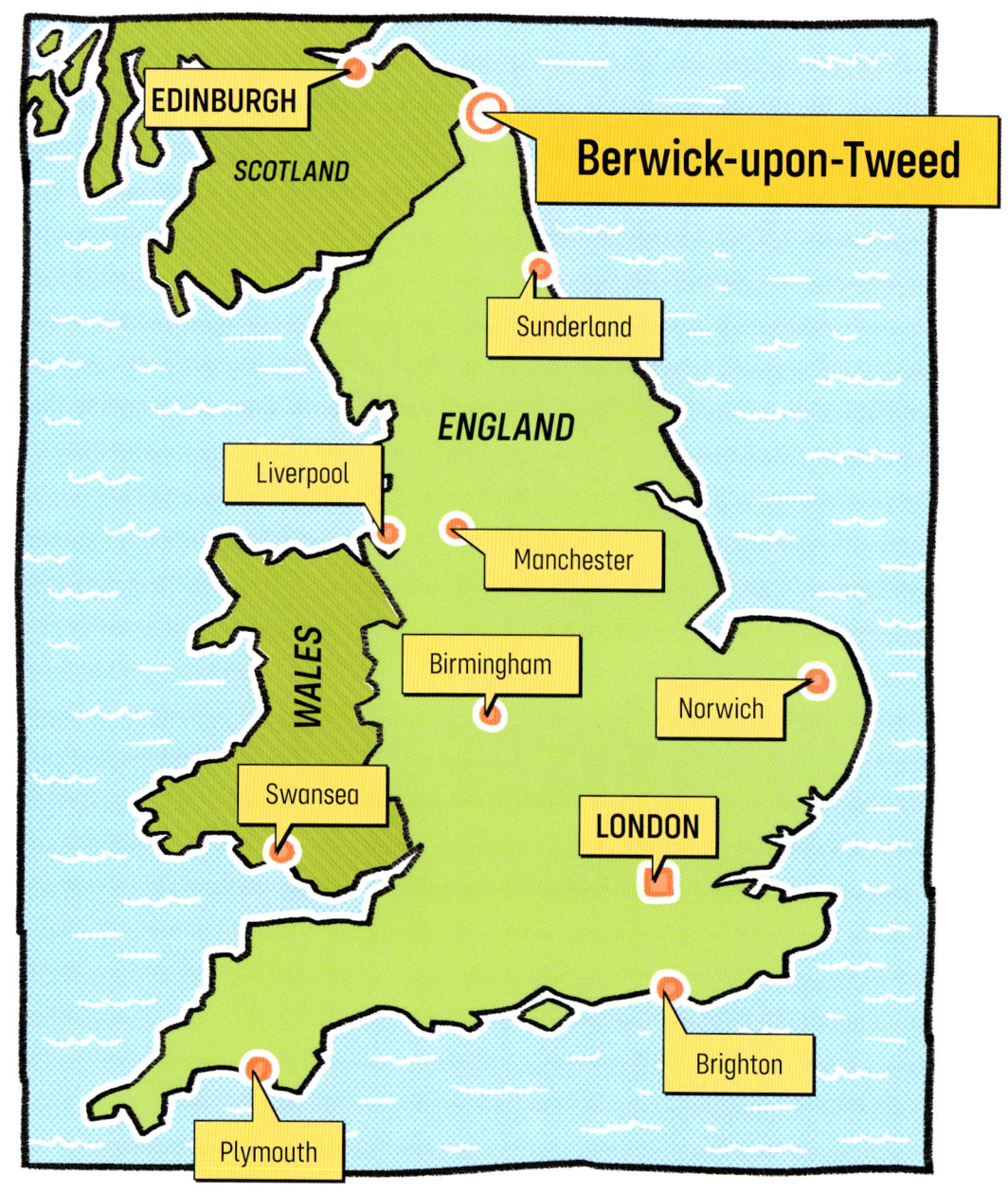

Lucy was born in 1991 in Berwick-upon-Tweed, which is England's most northern town. It's very close to the border of Scotland.

For a time, Lucy's family lived on the island of Lindisfarne.
It's a wild place where not many people live.

Also known as **Holy Island**

Lucy lived with her parents, Joaquin and Diane, her older brother, Jorge, and her younger sister, Sophie. Her dad is from Portugal.

Lucy was a very active little girl. She could ride a bike when she was two, and she loved joining in with anything her big brother did – including playing FOOTBALL!

Lucy was really good at football. She could run with the ball, score goals, and she wasn't afraid to tackle.

Lucy was shy at school. She didn't like putting her hand up in class or meeting new people.

But on the football pitch, Lucy felt confident. She was part of a team and a game she loved.

Lucy was very competitive and always wanted to win. She even cut her hair short so it would stop getting in the way when she played football.

Lucy's brother, Jorge, played for their local football club, Alnwick Town. When she was six, Lucy joined the club, too.

"GO LUCY!"

Lucy's mum and Auntie Julie took her to training and matches.

Lucy was the only girl in the team, but soon she was winning the tackles against the boys.

"WAAAH!"

When she was 12, Lucy was told she couldn't play in the boys' team anymore. So she joined the football academy at Sunderland football club, which was 50 miles away.

Lucy made it into Sunderland's first team when she was 16 and she became the team captain. In her first season, she was named the Manager's Player of the Year!

Lucy spent eight years with Sunderland. Her friend Lucy Staniforth was there, too!

Lucy was also called up to play for the England under-17 team.

It was a huge honour.

When she was 17, Lucy was asked to study and play football at the University of North Carolina. She jumped at the chance!

The USA is the top country for women's football, and Lucy was going to play for one of best university teams in the country: the North Carolina Tar Heels.

Many brilliant women footballers have played for the team, including the England coach Sarina Wiegman.

After a year in the USA, Lucy returned to England, but back home she suffered a serious knee injury.

Lucy was on crutches for a long time and spent a lot of time in hospitals having knee operations.

Lucy worked hard at university. To earn money, she worked at a pizza takeaway and in a café.

WHOAH!

But all Lucy really wanted to do was play football. She used her new sports science knowledge to create her own exercise programme to heal her knee injury.

Soon, Lucy was fully fit again! She started playing for Everton in the Women's Super League – the top league for women's football in England.

After two seasons at Everton, Lucy switched to their biggest rivals: Liverpool.

It was a good move for Lucy – she won the Women's Super League TWICE! She also won an award for Women's Players' Player of the Year.

Lucy joined Manchester City in 2015. With Lucy in defence, teams found it tough to score against them!

In 2017 Lucy moved to the French football club Lyon. They are one of the best sides in the world.

Lucy played amazing football at Lyon and even picked up the Best FIFA Women's Player award in 2020! She was the first British footballer ever to win it.

After that, she returned to Manchester City for a while, before heading off on a new adventure in 2022 to Barcelona in Spain, where she helped them to win the Champions League twice!

Bronze came back to England to play for Chelsea in 2024.

Lucy has also shown the world how good she is as an England player.

She reached the semi-finals of the World Cup twice, in 2015 and 2019.